S.E. LOUISIANA

showing a few of the

PLANTATION HOUSES

BATON RO...

Bringier

Oak Alley

Evergreen

LAKE MAUREPAS

LAKE PONTCHARTRAIN

Ormond

BAYOU LAFOURCHE

LAKE SALVADOR

Seven Oaks

NEW ORLEANS

Three Oaks

Rene Beauregard

MISSISSIPPI RIVER

BARATARIA BAY

PEARL RIVER

LAKE BORGNE

MISSISSIPPI SOUND

CHANDELEUR SOUND

FRONTISPIECE

Oldest Existing Structure in the Mississippi Valley   *Date 1727*

MADAM JOHN'S LEGACY, VIEUX CARRÉ

NEW ORLEANS
AND ITS ENVIRONS

THE DOMESTIC ARCHITECTURE

1727-1870

BY

ITALO WILLIAM RICCIUTI

PHOTOGRAPHS

BY

RUDOLF HERTZBERG

With an Introduction by

TALBOT FAULKNER HAMLIN

BONANZA BOOKS
NEW YORK

INTRODUCTION

NEW ORLEANS is unique among the cities of the United States. Climate and history have combined to make its people and its life different from those of other towns, and its architecture, always a sensitive expression of both factors, has necessarily developed its own characteristic forms, full of a special flavor. Yet, until now, these forms have remained largely unpublished. Nathaniel Courtland Curtis has brilliantly sketched the architectural history of New Orleans, in *New Orleans, Its Old Houses, Shops, and Public Buildings* (Philadelphia and London, J. B. Lippincott Co., 1933), but the limitations in a book of that kind prevented the extensive illustration of details necessary to give the architect and the interested layman a comprehensive knowledge of the forms themselves. This book of Mr. Ricciuti, with photographs by Rudolf Hertzberg, thus comes at a peculiarly opportune time, and for the first time through its pages the reader may gain an adequate idea of the real architectural wealth which New Orleans contains. It is an admirable complement to Mr. Curtis's work; in addition, its myriad pictures contain a vast fund of information and inspiration in themselves.

New Orleans was the country's first melting pot. French, Spanish, French again, and finally American, it has received gifts from many peoples and cultures. Yet both Spaniard and Frenchman built with such a sure eye to its climate and site and conditions, that it is always definitely American. Its Cabildo (built in 1795) may resemble the motives and the proportions shown in the drawings for the Casas Reales at Antequera in Mexico (1781) preserved in the archives of the the Indies in Seville; but the same archives show a military commander's house in Baton Rouge (1788), which, in its wide-spreading verandah and hipped and gabled roofs, is a characteristic Louisiana form. Similarly, the old Ursuline Convent, later used as an archbishopric, finished in 1734, may recall to us the gracious buildings of many a provincial French town; yet the early French houses, in their windows, their stairs, and their arrangements, are at least as American—or, rather as New Orleans-like—as they are French. You will find here neither the Spanish Baroque of Spain or Mexico, nor the manoirs and hotels of France; instead, the place from the very beginning stamped upon its buildings its own special character, from the small, one-story houses built in stuccoed half-timber, to the later high fronts gay with scrolled iron-work.

The same thing happened when, after New Orleans had become a part of the United States, immigrants poured into it from the North and the East. New Orleans was a dream city, then; cotton trade was booming, population was growing by leaps and bounds; despite floods and yellow fever, the flood of wealth was more important, the economic exuberance more attractive. Yet, as men from New England, New York, the entire Atlantic Seaboard came in on the tall ships that lay along the levees, as men from western Pennsylvania and Ohio and Illinois came floating down the river, the locality placed its stamp on them quite as much as they changed it, and though the front of the Grima house, built in 1830, has the red brick walls, the many-paned windows, and the white door of far-away New England or New York, its plan and its appointments are those of the regular New Orleans house. Each of these waves, and each of these peoples left a solid residue in architectural form, as they did in the population of the city, so that no other city anywhere has its character.

One examining these photographs is surprised, first, I think, by the strong "colonial" and classic revival character of the architectural detail. Two terrible fires, one in 1788 and one in 1794, account partly for this, for they swept away much of the early Spanish and French Building, so that the city today, even in its older parts, is the product largely of the American period since 1813, and the whole Garden District dates almost entirely from the great cotton boom days of 1830-1850. One enters an oval arched passage that gives a view of an almost tropical court beyond; the door through which one passes may have the delicate leaded side-lights and fan-lights of the North. Within, in the cool high living rooms, one comes with surprise upon a mantel which might grace a house in Massachusetts or early Ohio. On Chartres and on Royal Streets are houses the fronts of which—save for the ubiquitous balconies— might be found in Greenwich Village. Even in the cast iron work, so famous as to make the name, "New Orleans", almost synonymous with its lacy elegance, study reveals again and again motives identical with those of Charleston, Philadelphia, or New York.

There are two chief reasons for these similarities: the settling in New Orleans of architects and builders with a northern background, and the importation and wide use of such builders' and architects' handbooks as those of Benjamin and Lafever. A characteristic case is that of James Gallier, Senior. Born in Ireland, trained as builder and architect in Ireland and England, he came to New York in the spring, 1832, and worked as an architect and draftsman there, and in Boston, for some two and a half years; for one of these he was a partner of Minard Lafever. Disappointed in the opportunities offered in New York, he went to New Orleans in the fall of 1834, and rapidly became one of its busiest and most prosperous architects, the designer, for instance, of the City Hall. His son followed him, and between the two the Gallier family contributed not a little to the appearance of New Orleans. Through Gallier, moreover, the Dakin family came to New Orleans. James Dakin had been a pupil, and later a partner of Alexander Jackson Davis in New York, where Gallier had made his acquaintance, and he, like Gallier, had a son who followed him in the profession. Thus these two families, with training and background English and northern, joined with the French de Pouilly and the Freret family in making New Orleans what it is.

The evidence of the use of the architectural handbooks of Benjamin and Lafever —especially the latter—is wide-spread. Mantels, door, window, and dormer details, decorative plasterwork can again and again be traced to plates in these works. Some of the marble mantels are so similar, in fact, to mantels in New York, that one is led to wonder whether or not they were imported, ready-made, from some outside source, on the northern seaboard; or whether both northern and southern examples came from the same European manufactory, and the books merely copied them. Some of the cast iron balcony work may also have been shipped from the north, from one of several northern foundries; but we know that much of it was cast locally from patterns or sections of the work brought in from elsewhere.

Thus, out of the combined influences of France, Spain, England, New England and New York, New Orleans developed that peculiar and characteristic architectural expression which forms so great a part of its charm. It is good to have these New Orleans buildings and their details at last so carefully photographed. This book is a valuable record of a unique city and a unique portion of American culture.

TALBOT HAMLIN
Columbia University

AUTHOR'S FOREWORD

O BOOK using New Orleans either as background or principal theme has ever been able to escape its architecture. Yet, up to now no book has appeared which has done for the unique old architecture of this city that which has been done for the remains of the old buildings of other places. No previous attempt has been made to present an illustrated record of this architecture for use as a reference work for architects and draftsmen.

Being an architect, the lack of such a work was doubly noticeable to me, and resolving that something could be done about it, I began the task of gathering material —a task which would have been undertaken with reluctance had it not been for the encouragement and help received from the publishers of this book. Once begun, a sense of duty and a sort of patriotism had often to be called on to bolster up drooping enthusiasm as the months went by and the material accumulated, oh so slowly.

In gathering the material into book form, the reference character of the work was kept constantly in mind. Only buildings and details which possessed architectural merit were included, little or no attention being paid to historical, romantic or literary connections; consequently many buildings which are the mecca of visitors and tourists were omitted. Also, in an effort to cater to the contemporary interest in small buildings and dwellings and in order to keep the volume down to a reasonable size, concentration was almost entirely on structures of a non-public nature.

For easy reference it was believed feasible to keep photographs of building exteriors separate from various details such as iron work, doors, staircases, etc. Measured drawings of several of the illustrations found in the earlier pages have been placed at the end of the book. This arrangement has one disagreeable feature, the scattering of various parts of one building throughout the book. Chances are, however, that details of a specific kind will be more in demand than all the details of any one house. Nevertheless, whenever such a scattering occurs, attention is always called to those plates which illustrate other parts of the same building. Details have been arranged in chronological sequence as much as possible so that development and evolution may be traced. As for the exteriors of buildings they have inevitably fallen into three main groups, so sharp is the definition separating them. Occasional overlapping of one group into another exists but is always of minor importance, New Orleans having been saved for the most part from that ingrowing development which throttled the historic architecture of so many American cities. These three main groups—The Vieux Carré, The Garden District, and the Plantations—have been arranged as nearly as possible in their natural order of evolution. It is hoped that the following of the very obvious architectural development from page to page will give as much pleasure as was found in weighing the value of and judging the evidence which established precedence of one building over another.

All of the photographs shown herein were taken expressly for this purpose by Mr. Hertzberg. Mr. Hertzberg's help was invaluable also in the preparation of the measured drawings.

The great majority of the measured drawings were taken from the valuable material gathered by the Louisiana Division of the Historic American Building Survey and made available through the courtesy of Mr. Richard Koch of this city, director of the project. Mr. Koch's kindness saved much time and work and knowing the care and thoroughness with which the project under his direction is being carried out there was not the slightest hesitancy in accepting the authenticity of whatever material was used.

I am also greatly indebted to Mr. Nathaniel Courtland Curtis and his book, *New Orleans, Its Old Houses, Shops and Public Buildings*. I am so much in sympathy with Mr. Curtis's opinions that it is suspected that many of the ideas which I believe to be my own are actually more his than mine, or at least have their roots well planted in his writings and teachings.

Mr. Stanley Clisby Arthur's recent book on New Orleans has also proved invaluable. This work, result of painstaking study of notarial records, will inevitably be consulted by anyone whose interest lies in the architecture of the "French Quarter", as the Vieux Carré is called by New Orleanians.

Finally, in giving thanks, Mr. Hertzberg and I would be definite in assigning the place of honor to those good and courteous people who allowed us to photograph and measure their houses. Any hospitality which can still be gracious in the face of such utter disregard for the privacy and sanctity of the home, moving of furniture, strewing of electric wires and floodlights, removal of pictures and hangings, blocking of doorways and general disruption of the quiet and peace, deserves far greater reward than can possibly be satisfied by the mere mention of gratitude.

New Orleans—1938   ITALO WILLIAM RICCIUTI

GENERAL DESCRIPTION

WHEN in 1718, he was confronted with the need of a new trading post for John Law's *Compagnie de l'Occidente*, Jean Baptiste de Bienville found that the site upon which was to grow the city of New Orleans presented several distinct advantages. Three were of great importance; it possessed that which was lacking in the sticky morass which was most of South Louisiana, dry ground; it was accessible by two waterways, the Bayou St. John and the more dangerous Mississippi River; and the fact that the spot was well known to the Indians of the surrounding country as the home of the Houmas, making it excellent trading ground for the *Compagnie* just granted a twenty-five year charter of free trade in the province by the Duc d' Orleáns, regent of France.

Fifty men, under Sieur Le Blonde de la Tour, cleared and laid out the town—in rectangles, barely more than 100 in number. In the center facing the Mississippi and commanding the magnificent view which the broad sweep of the river gives at this point, was placed the town square later called the *Place d'Armes*, still later *Jackson Square*, the vandals of commerce and politics having long since substituted railroad tracks and dirty wharf sheds for vista and cool breezes. To the rear of the square was to be the church, the school and the government house.

The first houses were rudely built of split cypress slabs and palmetto thatched. Only rarely were clay plastered logs used. A sandy clay found along the banks of the river soon served for the manufacture of a soft brick, easily crushed. The weakness of the early brickwork led to the then rampant *Briqueté entre Poteaux* construction shown on Plate 1. In this type of construction a framework of heavy cypress timbers, giving structural stability to the building, was filled in solid with the soft brick. There are some examples of this "half-timber" mode of building which used adobe instead of brick for the filling in. The soft brick which eroded so easily was bonded by a mortar made from lime secured from clam shells found in nearby Lake Pontchartrain and the numerous bayous in the vicinity—this mortar, excellent if kept dry, becomes chalky and useless if exposed to the weather. The problem was solved by covering the brickwork with a coating of plaster. The same plaster covers the majority of brick buildings of the Vieux Carré today—for later when brick and mortar were of more durable character the habit of plastering brick walls had become so firmly rooted that to leave brickwork uncovered was tantamount to leaving a building naked.

NEW ORLEANS AND ITS ENVIRONS

The later buildings of the first French domination were usually one story, built flush with the sidewalk, and had wide projecting roof overhangs protecting sidewalks from the rain and glaring sun. The rooms facing the street were occupied by the shop of the business man who lived with his family in the rear or in a wing which flanked the small secluded court. Later the introduction of dormer windows made it possible for the heretofore waste space under the sloping roof to be used for living quarters.

In 1768, over the protest and rebellious objections of the French colonials much of Louisiana, including New Orleans, was turned over to Spain, Louis XV in a secret treaty six years before having ceded the territory to his cousin Charles III of Spain. This change so despised by the colonials was nevertheless the signal for a decided freshness in the architecture of the town. Permission of free trade with France and the American Colonies did much to bring money into the city and consequently stimulate building. Houses for the first time looked toward an occasional comfort outside the purely rudimentary necessity for shelter. Slight ornamentation became apparent in cornices and after the addition of dormers they too came to be outlined by mouldings Later these dormers became full second stories, low-ceilinged as yet, but serving to give better accommodations as living quarters. Thus the architecture of New Orleans began to come of age.

But it was actually the disastrous fires of 1788 and 1794, razing more than nine hundred buildings, which gave the greatest impetus to building. Unfortunate as those fires were to archaeology (they all but wiped out the old town) the building reforms and their stimulus to build in an entirely new manner proved invaluable in the architectural development of the city. Moreover wealth was accumulating, for New Orleans was now growing rapidly in importance as a commercial port through the development of the Middle West. Heretofore construction had more or less followed French colonial habits even into the Spanish era. Now, however, over the smoking ruins of the burned city appeared an architecture whose paved courtyards, massive arched doorways with their ponderous doors, iron-barred windows and wrought-iron balconies had a Spanish flavor which went well with the French heritage and the colonial exigencies of the place. Professional and business men of the community soon had the ostentation to build full two story and two story and a half houses. They still found it convenient to keep to the old plan of making their places of business and their residences in one building, but a more gracious social life among the colonials demanded that greater attention be paid to those rooms to be used for receiving and entertaining.

The primitiveness of the buildings slowly and surely disappeared, until the turn into the nineteenth century—when New Orleans was undergoing an astonishing change from Spanish to French and finally into American hands all within three years —saw the city standing on the threshold of an architectural development which within thirty years blossomed into a robust style, unique, truly indigenous. A style which can be called neither French nor Spanish nor Colonial even though these three influences are strongly distinguishable. The mannerisms of these three influences were combining into attitudes so strongly defined as to mark a truly independent style, an architecture whose determining factors were not traditional nor romantic but were those very factors which have always been the springboard of great architecture; climatological conditions, topography, local materials, and the social customs and cultural tastes of the times.

The chief factor was climate. New Orleans has a nine-month summer with predominant southeast moisture-laden breezes contributing to a humid subtropical climate. The winters are mild, slight freezes occurring about three times a year. For these general conditions the houses of this period were excellently suited. Courtyards shaded by high brick walls and wide-spreading banana leaves; cooling draughts through lofty-arched carriage drives; wide fanlight windows admitting the river breezes through broad halls and high-ceilinged rooms; long "galleries" shielding from the intense glare and thick brick walls excluding the heat of the street; everything was calculated to cool and refresh.

In plan the more important mansions followed fairly closely a single scheme. The main wing faced the street and contained on the ground floor the shop or counting room and above, the apartment of the owner. An arched flagstoned carriage drive flanking the shop led from the street to the courtyard. To one side and at the end of this passageway an open arcaded vestibule gave access to the gracefully sweeping staircase leading to the well-proportioned rooms of the floor above. At the head of the stairs an ample stairhall landing, enriched by wide fanlight windows, looked down on the brick or flagstone paved courtyard with its low bordering flower beds abundant in subtropical plants and its small cast iron fountain splashing cooly in the shade of oleander and camphor trees. It is here in these Vieux Carré courtyards that the Spanish were most successful in breaking through the stubbornness of French influence on the architecture of the city—a stubbornness which prevails to the present day.

On the rear of the main wing and extending along one side of the courtyard was the *garçonnière;* a name which came to be given because of its function as quarters for the younger members of the family and their friends and to take care of whatever overflow of guests there was from the main house. The *garçonnière* was always of two and sometimes three floors, each with its balcony overlooking the court, these floors seldom on the same level as those of the main house. The connection between the two was effected by means of little runs of stairs. The ground floor of this wing was given over to kitchen, service rooms and stables.

Entrance to the carriage passageway was through a massive door with hand-wrought hinges and cast knocker. A small door cut in one of the leaves of this large door was used for ordinary occasions when the full opening of the door was not only unnecessary but cumbersome.

The façades, setting flush with the sidewalks, were simple but excellently proportioned and of good scale, great care always being taken in the disposition of openings. The usual smoothly troweled plaster predominated in wall finishes. Long balconies, or "galleries" as they are called in the city, ran the full width of the building at the principal floor level. The supporting brackets, the railings and watershed supports of these balconies were of beautifully wrought iron often of decided Spanish pattern. Monograms together with other indentifying marks of the owner were cleverly interwoven into geometrical and stylized floral designs. The early wrought iron was imported, possibly from Spain, there being no then known deposits of iron ore in the vicinity. Much later local craftsmen began to work iron comparable to the imported product. Up to this time the use of cast iron for "galleries" was negligible. Later, after about 1830, the material came into such popularity that it is no exaggeration to say that buildings had "cast iron façades", as one authority puts it. Even though the effect of all this cast iron, such a distinguishing feature of old New Orleans architecture, is generally pleasing in its often-mentioned "lace-like" appearance, it can hardly be compared with the earlier wrought iron for sheer beauty and grace of design. Early architects achieved, however, extremely happy effects in cast iron by using motifs inspired by the luxuriant plant life of their own climate. The live oak, the rose vine and the morning glory are only a few among the infinite variety of designs produced at this time.

The consistent growth of the city meanwhile had caused more and more important houses to be built on the very fringe of the old town, along Rampart, Esplanade and Canal Streets. Numerous fortune-seeking Americans, lured by the advantageous situation of the city and the stories of fabulous riches and pleasures, began to settle in New Orleans. The antipathy of the Creoles to the newcomers caused most of these Americans to settle on the upstream side of the town in what was then the Faubourg Ste. Marie, and by 1850 many mansions had been built on the American side of Canal Street. With the pre-civil war prosperity of 1850-60 came a great boom for this section, later known as the Garden District. By this time, too, the wave of classical interest which had carried the Greek Revival on its crest had broken over the entire cultural element of the city. Two architects, a Frenchman, J. N. B. de

NEW ORLEANS AND ITS ENVIRONS

Pouilly, and an Irishman, James Gallier, Sr., were doing the most distinguished work. To the latter can be attributed much of the finest Greek Revival architecture in the city. The houses along Esplanade and Rampart Streets as well as several within the confines of the old square itself now assumed a different character. Cast iron was everywhere, covering the entire faces and much of the sides of buildings, Greek motifs being used extensively in their design. Great pains were taken in the correct use of the orders in the design of doorways. In the detailing of cornice mouldings great care was taken to adhere to Greek profiles. Brick was still the favorite material and plaster covered the surface of most of the "Creole" buildings. The influence of the Georgian architecture of the eastern states was asserting itself strongly, however, and many of the new buildings displayed many characteristics which cannot be called indigenous to New Orleans. Among these was the practice of leaving brick exposed.

The houses, used entirely as residences now, were larger, their principal floor raised from two to five feet above the street level. Small runs of stone steps led to the sidewalk through a small vestibule, open and re-entrant, in the face of the building. Generally an "L" in plan, the principal wing on the street rose higher than the service wing to the rear.

The interiors contained rooms of almost monumental proportions. Three elements were given great prominence on the first floor: the staircase, usually placed opposite the entrance door and at the end of the central hall; the double parlor, rooms identical in treatment and separated by a massive set of paneled sliding doors; and the carved marble mantels which graced every room in the house save those used for servants. Treatment of the bed rooms of the second floor was almost as careful as that accorded the parlors and dining room on the first floor. Cornices were always accented with plaster mouldings. The center of the ceilings of the more important rooms were invariably enriched by well designed rosettes of plaster. Doors and windows were treated alike, the window casings carrying clear to the floor with a panel treatment under the sill. The deep reveals of window openings often ingeniously concealed shutters which folded back out of sight when not in use.

Floors were usually of wide planks of pine or cypress painted a dark brown which became almost black with frequent polishing.

In plot plan the houses of the Garden District differed somewhat from those of other sections built during the same period. Being blessed with more room they usually were set far back from the property lines leaving areas for large informally planned gardens and lawns, usually on fills about one foot or so above the level of the sidewalk. The bases of stone walls or iron fences did double duty as retaining walls for these fills. Cast iron was used extensively and here gained its most intelligent function. The plant motifs of the designs made an excellent and admirable transition from the walls of the buildings to the foliage of the surrounding gardens. The result was a complete wedding of the house to its *entourage*. Large "galleries", one for each floor, covered the entire front and back and occasionally part of the sides of the building. These "galleries" were supported either by cast iron panels or by doric pilasters the full height of the façade. This latter, however, was properly a development of the plantation type of house which had an evolution all its own.

During the early days of the city a small settlement sprang up around the boat landing on Bayou St. John. Large plantations lined the banks, plantations which have long since been subdivided into city blocks, leaving the residences of their owners standing disconsolate among puny neighbors. These houses, with their broad verandahs and high hipped roofs, have a peculiar West Indian aspect, possibly dictated by the memories carried to New Orleans by immigrants many of whom came from the West Indies. Whatever the reason, the plan and arrangements of these houses were admirably suited to the climate and to the exigencies of plantation life. Of two stories they followed the Latin custom of placing the important floor on the second level, the ground floor serving the approximate functions of a basement. Hipped roofs extended over the broad "galleries" or verandas which often completely surrounded the house. Small turned wooden columns with square base and capitals supported the overhang. These columns were set over the large plaster-covered brick piers, either square or round, of the ground floor.

Usually staircases were on the inside and given a prominent place in the plan. The rooms of the principal floor above were of stately and elegant proportions, numerous French doors opening onto the "galleries" being the only windows in most of the rooms.

The "raised basement" of this type of house shared with several examples in the "Quarter" and the Garden District in giving to New Orleans a development uniquely indigenous. The water-soaked condition of the soil made the building of subsurface basements an impracticable procedure. The problem was solved by raising the whole house to allow room for a basement above the ground level. Several examples still stand today in every section of the city which date from the earliest times of New Orleans. In the "Quarter", Madam John's Legacy, illustrated in the frontispiece, the so-called "Beauregard House", Plate 16, and the house on Dauphine Street whose iron ballustraded staircase is shown on Plate 55, are the principal examples. In the Garden

District, Madam Chaffraix's House, Plate 32, the Maginnis House, Plate 28, and indeed most of the houses in the section are raised considerably above the ground. Of the latter plantations, the Hurst Plantation, now the Ike Stauffer home, illustrated in several plates of this book, is the outstanding example. It is this characteristic which marks the chief difference between the plantation houses of Louisiana and those of the northeast states of Southern tradition where the plantation houses had their principal floor at the ground level or very nearly so.

Later, plantation houses in Louisiana, influenced by the Greek Revival and by the American influx, lost much of their original characteristics. In the vicinity of New Orleans several examples of plantation houses of the period of greatest development are standing. Usually of stately proportions these buildings have columns, generally plastered brick, extending two full floors. These columns often surrounded the building, Doric or Ionic capitals supporting the overhang of the roof which extended to shelter the second floor "gallery". Often a *belvedere* crowned the meeting of the roof hips coming from the four corners of the building.

In plan a centrally located hall extended from front to back on both floors. A mahogany handrailed staircase connected the two halls—if the staircase was on the interior. When outside stairs were used they were of simple design and usually led directly to a fine doorway at the front end of the second floor hall. The disposition of rooms followed fairly closely the same arrangement as the earlier houses mentioned above. Mantels, usually of marble, sometimes of wood, were delicately carved. The plaster cornices and center rosettes of the important rooms were of interesting profile of Greek derivation. Door and window casings were treated alike, wood paneling being used between the window sills and the floor. In the later examples the mouldings of the door and window cases represented intricately woven leaves and garlands making a framing of indescribable elegance.

By the 1860's cotton had completely supplanted the Port as New Orleans' chief economic reliance, the opening of the Erie Canal and the building of railroads having diverted tons of produce from the Middle West to the Atlantic Seaboard. But with the shift to cotton came absolute dependence on slavery and the surrender of New Orleans to the Federal Forces in the War of Secession in 1862 marked the end of the city's greatest period of prosperity. Perhaps it was just as well for already the dread symptoms of architectural decadence had begun to show themselves. Coarse detail and coarser ornament forecast the beginning of that period so aptly called by someone "the dark ages of American architecture", a period which New Orleans like most other American cities far from escaped. In the past few years, after three quarters of a century of "gingerbread" and "façade builders", it is gratifying to note the return to New Orleans of architecture which, though totally different in outward forms, seems to be motivated by the same simple formulas of living comfort which gave to the "Courtyard Houses" of the Vieux Carré, the houses of the Garden District and the Plantation Houses in the vicinity so much of their charm.

LIST OF PLATES
NEW ORLEANS AND ITS ENVIRONS

LIST OF PLATES

LIST OF PLATES

LIST OF PLATES

LIST OF PLATES

LIST OF PLATES

NOTE; All numbers on Plates refer to additional illustrations or drawings of the same subject.

PLATE 1

NEW ORLEANS AND ITS ENVIRONS

VIEUX CARRÉ

Typical "Briquete Entre Poteux" Construction
Measured Drawings, 118 and 119

Built sometime between 1772 and 1791

"LAFITTE'S BLACKSMITH SHOP"

Note Double Pitched Roof and Large Overhanging Eaves   *Late 18th Century*

DUMAINE STREET

This Cottage Has One of the Few Remaining Flat Tiled Roofs   *Late 18th Century*
Which, Shipped from Nantes, France, Were Used after the
Fires of 1788 and 1794

KERLEREC STREET

Cottage   *Late 18th Century*
Measured Drawing of Cornice, 134
ST. PHILIP STREET

Cottage   *Late 18th Century*
BURGUNDY STREET

PLATE 4

NEW ORLEANS AND ITS ENVIRONS

VIEUX CARRÉ

Cottage   Early 19th Century

DUMAINE STREET

Cottage   Late 18th Century

ST. PHILIP STREET

Note Typical Front and Back Sloped Roof Due to Necessity of Keeping Water
Out of Narrow Passageways between Buildings.

Cottage

Early Use of Arched Openings
DAUPHINE STREET

Note Transom Treatment

ST. PHILIP STREET

PLATE 6

NEW ORLEANS AND ITS ENVIRONS

VIEUX CARRÉ

Typical Story-and-One-Half Cottage of the Late 18th Century

ST. ANN STREET

Additional Illustration, 65

CHESNEAUX HOUSE

Date 1800

Example of Business-Residential Building

Additional Illustration 54

Built about 1801

"PATIO ROYAL"

PLATE 8

VIEUX CARRÉ

Date 1808

Built about 1806

Additional Illustration, 79

TYPICAL BUSINESS-RESIDENTIAL BUILDINGS

"ABSINTHE HOUSE"

MARCHAND HOUSE

PLATE 9

NEW ORLEANS AND ITS ENVIRONS

VIEUX CARRÉ

TYPICAL BUSINESS-RESIDENTIAL BUILDINGS

BARRACKS AND ROYAL STREET

TOULOUSE STREET

PLATE 10

NEW ORLEANS AND ITS ENVIRONS

VIEUX CARRÉ

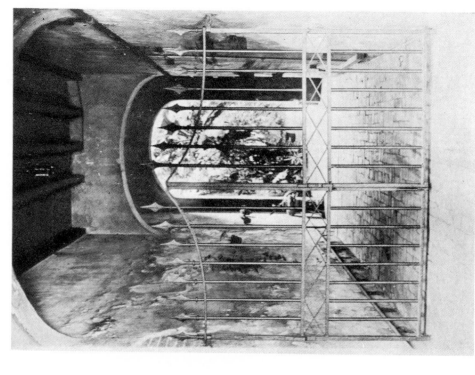

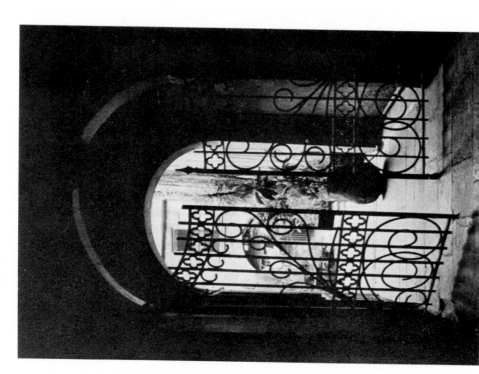

Additional Illustrations 11, 83 and 88
Drawings, 120, 121 and 133

TYPICAL PORTE-COCHÈRE ENTRANCES TO "COURTYARD HOUSE"

CASA FLINARD

ROYAL STREET

Early 19th Century   *Street Façade*   *Early 19th Century*

*Garçonnière, Rafter Ends and Steps to
Main Part of House*
Additional Illustrations, 10, 83 and 88
Drawings, 120, 121 and 133

CASA FLINARD   ROYAL STREET

Fanlight Windows Overlooking Courtyard   *Date 1813*

MAISON JACOB

These, with the Passageways and Courtyards Shown on the Facing Page, Are the
Ever-Present Elements of the "Courtyard House."

PLATE 12

NEW ORLEANS AND ITS ENVIRONS

First Half of 19th Century

ORLEANS STREET

VIEUX CARRÉ

"CONTRASTING TYPES OF GARÇONNIÈRES"

Built about 1822
Benjamin F. Fox, Arch.

TOULOUSE STREET

Garçonnière   *Built in the 1820's*
Additional Illustrations, 16, 17, 72, 86, 90, 97, 102 and 107

GRIMA HOUSE

Back of Main Building from Courtyard   *Built about 1801*

LANGUILLE HOUSE

PLATE 15

NEW ORLEANS AND ITS ENVIRONS

VIEUX CARRÉ

Built about 1798

Additional Illustrations, 54, 80, 89 and 109

GIROD HOUSE

Date 1821

Benjamin Henry Latrobe, Arch.

Additional Illustrations, 66 and 111

OLD LOUISIANA STATE BANK

Example of "Raised Cottage"   *Date 1826*
Additional Illustrations, 70 and 96   Francisco Correjolles, Arch.
Drawing, 128

"BEAUREGARD HOUSE"

Courtyard Kitchen   *Built in the 1820's*
Additional Illustrations, 13, 17, 72, 86, 90, 97, 102 and 107

GRIMA HOUSE

VIEUX CARRÉ

Rear of Main Building from Courtyard

Additional Illustrations, 13, 16, 72, 86, 90, 97, 102 and 107

Built in the 1820's

GRIMA HOUSE

Date 1835
Additional Illustration, 59

LE PRÉTE HOUSE

PLATE 19

NEW ORLEANS AND ITS ENVIRONS

VIEUX CARRÉ

Built about 1837

LA BRANCHE BUILDING

Date 1837

MILTENBERGER BUILDING

TYPICAL "CAST-IRON FAÇADES"

The "Eastern" Influence on the Greek Revival of the Old Quarter　　　　*Date 1838*
Additional Illustration, 113

"LE PETIT SALON"

VIEUX CARRÉ

BOURBON STREET

BASIN STREET

Additional Illustration, 74

Two Greek Revival Buildings on the Fringe of the Old Quarter; Note the Contrast between the "Eastern" Type on the Left and the More "Creole" Treatment on the Right.

Typical Two and One-Half Story Buildings
Built about 1840

ESPLANADE AVENUE

Typical Two Story House   *Mid 19th Century*

COLISEUM STREET

Date 1856

Additional Illustration, 60

THE GAUCHE HOUSE

Typical Two Story House
Additional Illustration, 77

FIRST STREET

Mid 19th Century
Additional Illustration, 78

LOGAN HOUSE

Attributed to James Gallier, Sr., Arch.

PLATE 26

NEW ORLEANS AND ITS ENVIRONS

GARDEN DISTRICT

Built about 1848

Another Type of Two Story House
Additional Illustrations, 77, 100 and 101

FORSYTH RESIDENCE

Typical Two Story House

ST. CHARLES AVENUE

GARDEN DISTRICT

Example of "Raised Cottage"

MAGINNIS RESIDENCE

GARDEN DISTRICT

Example of "Raised Cottage"

DAMERON HOUSE

Side View of Main Building   *Date 1870*
Additional Illustrations, 31, 62 and 87   James Freret, Arch.

BRADISH JOHNSON HOUSE

Servants' Wing   *Date 1870*
                                                   James Freret, Arch.

BRADISH JOHNSON HOUSE

Garden Wall   *Date 1870*
Additional Illustrations, 30, 62 and 87   James Freret, Arch.

BRADISH JOHNSON HOUSE

GARDEN DISTRICT

Example of "Raised Cottage"
Additional Illustration, 117

Built in the Late 1860's

MADAM CHAFFRAIX'S HOME

Date 1864
Additional Illustrations, 61, 83, 87, 93, 103 and 117   Attributed to James Gallier, Jr., Arch.

ROBINSON HOUSE

Typical Bayou St. John Dwelling   *Built about 1784*

"SPANISH CUSTOM HOUSE"

PLATE 35

NEW ORLEANS AND ITS ENVIRONS

THE PLANTATIONS

Early 19th Century

DUCAYET HOUSE

Typical Bayou St. John Dwelling

THE PLANTATIONS

More Pretentious Bayou St. John Dwelling
Additional Illustration, 70

Early 19th Century

BLANC HOUSE

THE PLANTATIONS

Although This Building Is Actually Situated in the Garden District
It Originally Served as a Plantation Overseer's House

Additional Illustration, 114
Drawing of Cornice, 134

THOMAS TOBY HOUSE

Built about 1830

Second Half 18th Century
Additional Illustration, 108
Measured Drawing of Dormer, 135

"DELOR SARPY", NEW ORLEANS

Built about 1803
Additional Illustration, 40   Wings added sometime between 1811 and 1819
Measured Drawings, 122, 123 and 127

"ORMOND", ST. CHARLES PARISH

Column Detail   *Mid 19th Century*

"ELMWOOD", HARAHAN

PLATE 40

THE PLANTATIONS

Additional Illustrations, 41 and 91
Measured Drawing, 129
"THREE OAKS," ST. BERNARD PARISH

Additional Illustrations, 38
Measured Drawings, 122, 123 and 127
"ORMOND," ST. CHARLES PARISH

Built about 1803

Contrasting Column Treatment; the "Eastern" Influence on the Left and the Typically Louisiana on the Right,
Probably Springing from West Indian Origins.

"THREE OAKS", ST. BERNARD PARISH

Additional Illustrations, 40 and 91
Measured Drawing, 129

A Remodeling of an Earlier House

"THE HERMITAGE", GEISMAR

Built in 1812

Date 1840

James Gallier, Sr., Arch.

"RENÉ BEAUREGARD", ST. BERNARD PARISH

PLATE 44

NEW ORLEANS AND ITS ENVIRONS

THE PLANTATIONS

"SEVEN OAKS", WESTWEGO

Date 1830

"EVERGREEN", WALLACE

Built about 1840

Front of Main Building   *Date 1830*

An "Eastern" Georgian House, Not Typical
of Louisiana Plantation Buildings

Additional Illustrations, 47, 83, 91, 97, 98, 107 and 113

"THE SHADOWS", NEW IBERIA

Facing Bayou Teche
Additional Illustrations, 46, 83, 91, 97, 98, 107 and 113

Date 1830

(The Central Portion Added about 30 Years Later.)

"THE SHADOWS", NEW IBERIA

Built 1837
Recently Restored

Additional Illustrations, 71, 85, 94, 106 and 115

"OAK ALLEY", DONALDSONVILLE

Built about 1832

Recently Moved from Its Original Site

"HURST", NEW ORLEANS

Additional Illustrations, 71, 104, 105, 107, 115 and 116

Pigeonnier   *Date 1836*

"UNCLE SAM", CONVENT

Date 1800

OLD GAZ BANK, VIEUX CARRÉ

Wrought Iron Balcony Details   *Date 1811*
Measured Drawing, 124

"FIRST SKYSCRAPER"

Date 1834

CASA CORREJOLLES, VIEUX CARRÉ

Note Masonic Emblem Over Monogram   *Wrought Iron Panel*
and Snakes Worked Into Side Panel   *Details on Balconies*

VIEUX CARRÉ

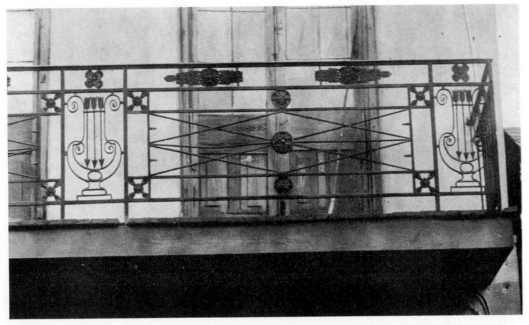

Early 19th Century

VIEUX CARRÉ

Combination Wrought and Cast Iron Balcony Details   *Early 19th Century*

VIEUX CARRÉ

PLATE 54

NEW ORLEANS AND ITS ENVIRONS

IRONWORK

Wrought Iron Bracket Details

House Illustrated, 15
Details, 80, 89 and 109

GIROD HOUSE, VIEUX CARRÉ

House Illustrated, 7

"PATIO ROYAL", VIEUX CARRÉ

Railing Detail   *Date 1851*
                                                        J. H. B. DuPouilly, Arch.

XIQUES HOUSE, VIEUX CARRÉ

Garde de Frise   *Railing Detail*

Early 19th Century

DEJEAN HOUSE, VIEUX CARRÉ

Rosette and Arrow Design

VIEUX CARRÉ

"Bow and Arrow" Design   *Combination Wrought and*
                                            Cast Iron Balcony Details

VIEUX CARRÉ

VIEUX CARRÉ

Interesting Imitation of Wrought Iron Mannerisms   *Cast Iron Balcony Details*
Additional Illustrations, 90 and 95

"CASA MIRO", VIEUX CARRÉ

PLATE 58

NEW ORLEANS AND ITS ENVIRONS

IRONWORK

Mid 19th Century

VIEUX CARRÉ

Cast Iron Panel Detail

PLATE 59

NEW ORLEANS AND ITS ENVIRONS

IRONWORK

Date 1835

House Illustrated, 18

LE PRÊTE HOUSE, VIEUX CARRÉ

Date 1851

James Gallier, Sr., Arch.

Cast Iron Balcony Details

PONTALBA BUILDING, VIEUX CARRÉ

House Illustrated, 23

Date 1856

GAUCHE HOUSE, VIEUX CARRÉ

Stable Gates   *Date 1864*
Additional Illustrations, 33, 87, 92, 93, 103 and 117   Attributed to James Gallier, Jr., Arch.

ROBINSON HOUSE, GARDEN DISTRICT

Entrance Gate and Wall   *Built about 1857*

VIEUX CARRÉ

Entrance Gate
Additional Illustrations, 30, 31 and 87

BRADISH JOHNSON HOUSE, GARDEN DISTRICT

Entrance Gate   *Built about 1850*

THE ROBB HOUSE, GARDEN DISTRICT

Entrance Door and Transom   *Late 18th Century*

VIEUX CARRÉ

Porte Cochère   *Date 1800*

Note Small Door for Use on Ordinary Occasions

House Illustrated, 6

CHESNEAUX HOUSE, VIEUX CARRÉ

DOORWAYS

VIEUX CARRÉ

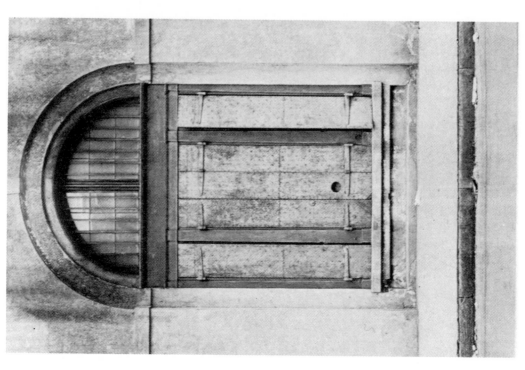

Date 1821

Building Illustrated, 15
Additional Illustration, 111

Benjamin Henry Latrobe, Arch.

OLD LOUISIANA STATE BANK, VIEUX CARRÉ

DOORWAYS

VIEUX CARRÉ

VIEUX CARRÉ

Portes Cochères, Early 19th Century

PLATE 68

NEW ORLEANS AND ITS ENVIRONS

Date 1811

VIEUX CARRÉ

DOORWAYS

Date 1834

Measured Drawings, 130 and 134

BRIGOT HOUSE, VIEUX CARRÉ

Date 1828

VIEUX CARRÉ

DOORWAYS

Early 19th Century

House Illustrated, 36

BLANC PLANTATION

Date 1826

House Illustrated, 16
Detail, 96
Measured Drawing, 128

"BEAUREGARD HOUSE", VIEUX CARRÉ

House Illustrated, 48
Additional Illustrations, 85, 94, 106 and 115

Date 1837

"OAK ALLEY"

House Illustrated, 49
Additional Illustrations, 104, 105, 107, 115 and 116

Built about 1832

HURST PLANTATION

Built in the 1820's

Additional Illustrations, 13, 16, 17, 86, 90, 97, 102 and 107

GRIMA HOUSE, VIEUX CARRÉ

PLATE 73

DOORWAYS

Date 1832

LA LAURIE HOUSE, VIEUX CARRÉ

Date 1857

GALLIER HOUSE, VIEUX CARRÉ

Built about 1840

Mid 19th Century

DOORWAYS

House Illustrated, 21

VIEUX CARRÉ

PLATE 75

NEW ORLEANS AND ITS ENVIRONS

DOORWAYS

VIEUX CARRÉ

Date 1836

Additional Illustration, 81

BIENVENUE HOUSE, VIEUX CARRÉ

2nd Half 19th Century

VIEUX CARRÉ

DOORWAYS

House Illustrated, 26
Additional Illustrations, 100 and 101

Built about 1848

FORSYTH RESIDENCE, GARDEN DISTRICT

House Illustrated, 24

GARDEN DISTRICT

Mid 19th Century

House Illustrated, 25   Attributed to James Gallier, Sr., Arch.

LOGAN HOUSE, GARDEN DISTRICT

Courtyard Stair to Apartments Above   *Date 1808*
House Illustrated, 8

MARCHAND HOUSE, VIEUX CARRÉ

Built about 1798

House Illustrated, 15
Additional Illustrations, 54, 89 and 109

GIROD HOUSE, VIEUX CARRÉ

Date 1836

Additional Illustration, 75

BIENVENUE HOUSE, VIEUX CARRÉ

PLATE 82

STAIRCASES

Built about 1795

LOUBIES HOUSE, VIEUX CARRÉ

PLATE 83

NEW ORLEANS AND ITS ENVIRONS

STAIRCASES

Date 1830

House Illustrated, 46 and 47
Additional Illustrations, 91, 97, 98, 107 and 113

"THE SHADOWS"

Early 19th Century

Additional Illustrations, 10, 11 and 88
Measured Drawings, 120, 121 and 133

CASA FLINARD, VIEUX CARRÉ

STAIRCASES

Entry and Porte Cochère Beyond

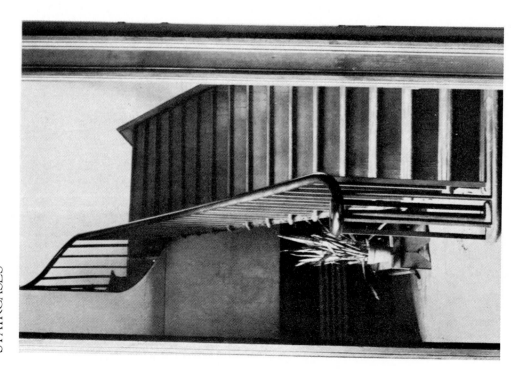

Newel and Turn
Additional Illustrations, 90, 96, 99 and 106

LABATUT—PUIG HOUSE, VIEUX CARRÉ
Date 1831

Two Views of Courtyard Staircase to Apartments above
(A Typical "Courtyard" House Staircase)

STAIRCASES

Newel

Date 1837

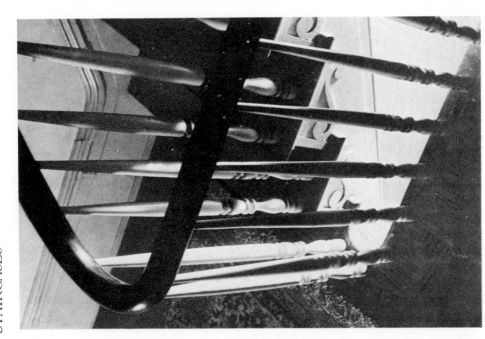

Stair Turn
House Illustrated, 48
Additional Illustrations, 71, 94, 106 and 115

Two Views of Interior Staircase
"OAK ALLEY"

PLATE 86

NEW ORLEANS AND ITS ENVIRONS

STAIRCASES

Late 18th Century

DESTREHAN PLANTATION

Built in the 1820's

Additional Illustrations, 13, 16, 17, 72, 90, 97, 102 and 107

GRIMA HOUSE, VIEUX CARRÉ

Interior Staircases

STAIRCASES

Date 1870

Additional Illustrations, 30, 31 and 62

James Freret, Arch.

BRADISH JOHNSON HOUSE, GARDEN DISTRICT

Date 1864

Additional Illustrations, 33, 61, 92, 93, 103 and 117

Attributed to James Gallier, Jr., Arch.

ROBINSON HOUSE, GARDEN DISTRICT

PLATE 88

NEW ORLEANS AND ITS ENVIRONS

INTERIORS

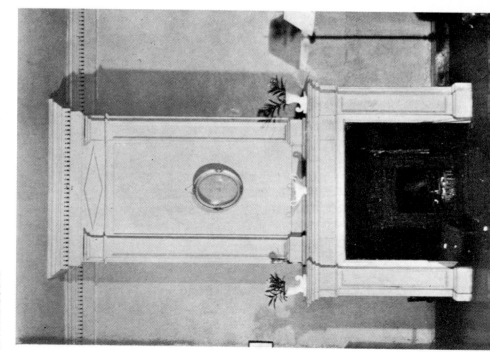

Additional Illustrations, 10, 11 and 83
Drawings, 120, 121 and 133

Drawing Room Mantels, Early 19th Century
CASA FLINARD, VIEUX CARRÉ

Drawing Room Mantel
House Illustrated, 15
Additional Illustrations, 54, 80 and 109

GIROD HOUSE, VIEUX CARRÉ

Early 19th Century

Note Cast Iron   *Date 1831*
LABUTUT—PUIG HOUSE
Additional Illustrations, 84, 96, 99 and 106

"CASA MIRO"
Additional Illustrations 57 and 95

Built in the 1820's
GRIMA HOUSE
Additional Illustrations, 13, 16, 17, 72, 86, 97, 102 and 107

TYPICAL MANTELS—VIEUX CARRÉ

Mantel   *Date 1830*
House Illustrated, 46 and 47
Additional Illustrations, 83, 97, 98, 107 and 113
               "THE SHADOWS"

Mantel
House Illustrated, 41
Additional Illustration, 40
Drawing, 129
            "THREE OAKS" PLANTATION

Bed Room Mantel   *Date 1864*

ROBINSON HOUSE, GARDEN DISTRICT

Dining Room Mantel   *Date 1864*

Additional Illustrations, 33, 61, 87, 93, 103 and 117

ROBINSON HOUSE, GARDEN DISTRICT

Library Mantel   *Date 1864*

Additional Illustrations, 33, 61, 87, 92, 103 and 117

ROBINSON HOUSE, GARDEN DISTRICT

Drawing Room Mantel   *Date 1864*

FRERET HOUSE, GARDEN DISTRICT

INTERIORS

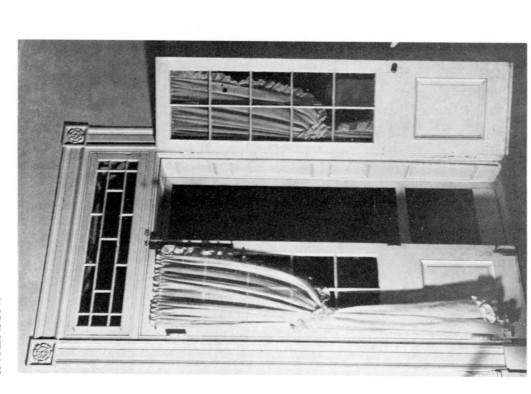

House Illustrated, 48
Additional Illustrations, 71, 85, 106 and 115

"OAK ALLEY"

Door and Transom Details

Additional Illustrations, 57, 90 and 95

"CASA MIRO" VIEUX CARRÉ

Door and Transom Details
"CASA MIRO", VIEUX CARRÉ

Additional Illustrations, 57, 90 and 94

Double-Parlor Door
Additional Illustrations, 84, 90, 99 and 106

LABATUT-PUIG HOUSE, VIEUX CARRÉ

Note Transom and Side-Light Treatment

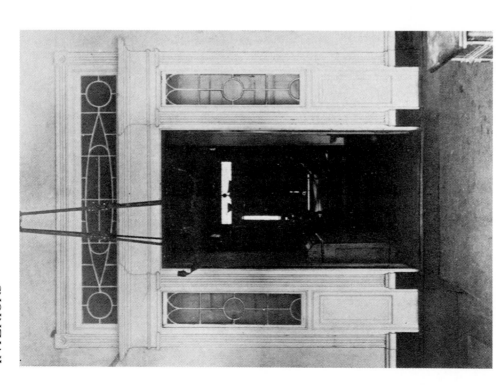

Door Detail
House Illustrated, 16
Additional Illustration, 70
Measured Drawing, 128

"BEAUREGARD HOUSE," VIEUX CARRÉ

INTERIORS

Additional Illustrations, 13, 16, 17, 72, 86, 90, 102 and 107

Double-Parlor Doors

GRIMA HOUSE, VIEUX CARRÉ

House Illustrated, 46 and 47
Additional Illustrations, 83, 91, 98, 107 and 113

"THE SHADOWS"

PLATE 98

NEW ORLEANS AND ITS ENVIRONS

INTERIORS

Double Parlor

House Illustrated, 46 and 47

Additional Illustrations, 83, 91, 97, 107 and 113

"THE SHADOWS"

INTERIORS

Double Parlor
Additional Illustrations, 84, 90, 96 and 106

LABATUT-PUIG HOUSE, VIEUX CARRÉ

Double Parlor
House Illustrated, 26
Additional Illustrations, 77 and 101

FORSYTH RESIDENCE, GARDEN DISTRICT

House Illustrated, 26
Additional Illustrations, 77 and 100

Door Details

FORSYTH RESIDENCE, GARDEN DISTRICT

PLATE 102

NEW ORLEANS AND ITS ENVIRONS

INTERIORS

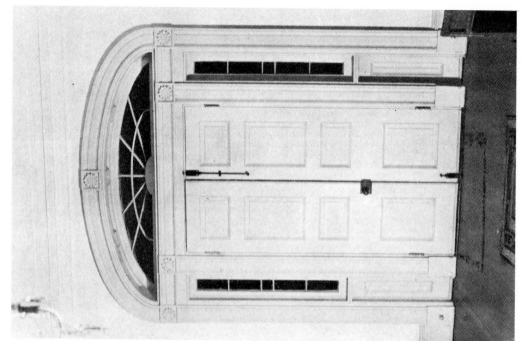

Entrance Door Detail

Door and Window Detail

Additional Illustrations, 13, 16, 17, 72, 86, 90, 97 and 107

GRIMA HOUSE, VIEUX CARRÉ

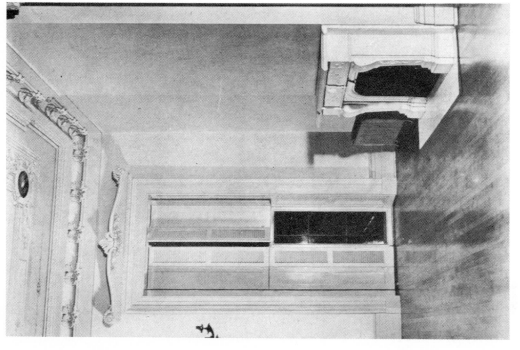

Curved Door in Stairhall

Additional Illustrations, 33, 61, 87, 92, 93 and 117

Corner of Drawing Room

ROBINSON HOUSE, GARDEN DISTRICT

INTERIORS

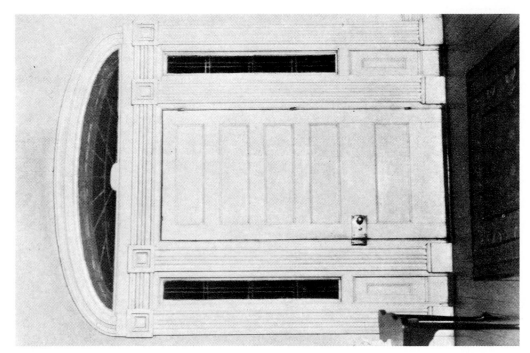

Entrance Door Detail

Window Detail
House Illustrated, 49
Additional Illustrations, 71, 105, 107, 115 and 116

HURST PLANTATION

PLATE 105

INTERIORS

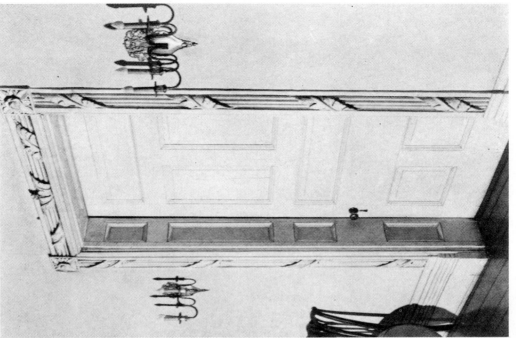

Door Detail

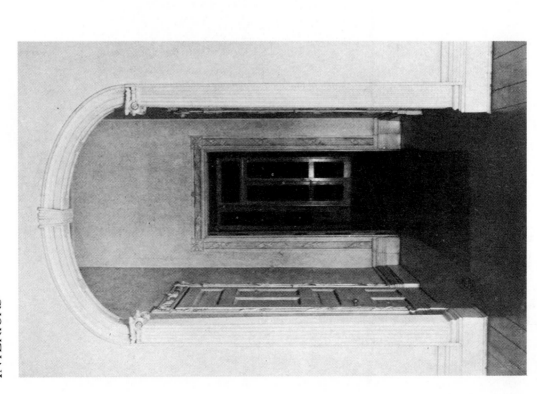

Hall
House Illustrated, 49
Additional Illustrations, 71, 104, 107, 115 and 116

HURST PLANTATION

INTERIORS

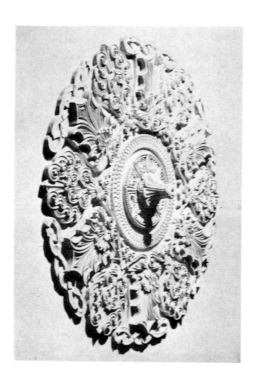

House Illustrated, 48
Additional Illustrations, 71, 85, 94 and 115

"OAK ALLEY"

Additional Illustrations, 84, 90, 96 and 99

Plaster Rosettes

LABATUT-PUIG HOUSE, VIEUX CARRÉ

Pilaster Cornice Detail

LABATUT-PUIG HOUSE, VIEUX CARRÉ

INTERIORS

House Illustrated, 49
Additional Illustrations, 71, 104, 105, 115 and 116

HURST PLANTATION

House Illustrated, 46 and 47
Additional Illustrations, 83, 91, 97, 98 and 113

"THE SHADOWS"

Additional Illustrations, 13, 16, 17, 72, 86, 90, 97 and 102

GRIMA HOUSE, VIEUX CARRÉ

"THE SHADOWS"

Plaster Cornice Details

House Illustrated, 38
Drawing, 135

VIEUX CARRÉ   DELOR SARPY PLANTATION

VIEUX CARRÉ

VIEUX CARRÉ

House Illustrated, 15
Additional Illustrations, 54, 80 and 89

GIROD HOUSE, VIEUX CARRÉ

PLATE 110

NEW ORLEANS AND ITS ENVIRONS

CORNICES AND DORMERS

Plaster-on-Brick Cornices

VIEUX CARRÉ

Building Illustrated, 15   Benjamin Henry Latrobe, Arch.
Additional Illustration, 66

OLD LOUISIANA BANK, VIEUX CARRÉ

PLATE 112

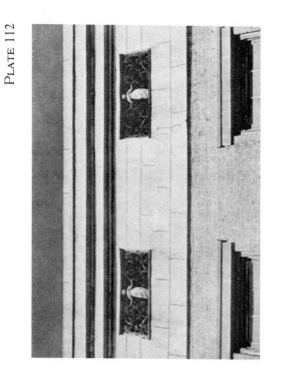

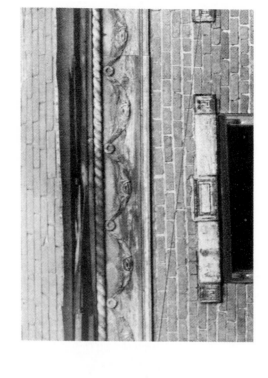

CORNICES AND DORMERS

VIEUX CARRÉ

CORNICES AND DORMERS

House Illustrated, 20

"LE PETIT SALON," VIEUX CARRÉ

Date 1830

Restored Recently
House Illustrated, 46 and 47
Additional Illustrations, 83, 91, 97, 98 and 107

"THE SHADOWS"

House Illustrated, 37
Drawing, 134

THOMAS TOBY PLANTATION

VIEUX CARRÉ

House Illustrated, 48
Additional Illustrations, 71, 85, 94 and 106

"OAK ALLEY"

House Illustrated, 49
Additional Illustrations, 71, 104, 105, 107 and 116

HURST PLANTATION

House Illustrated, 49
Additional Illustrations, 71, 104, 105, 107 and 115

HURST PLANTATION

CORNICES AND DORMERS   PLATE 117

Wood Cornice   *Cast Iron Balcony*
Additional Illustrations, 33, 61, 87, 92, 93 and 103

ROBINSON HOUSE, GARDEN DISTRICT

House Illustrated, 32

MADAM CHAFFRAIX'S HOME, GARDEN DISTRICT

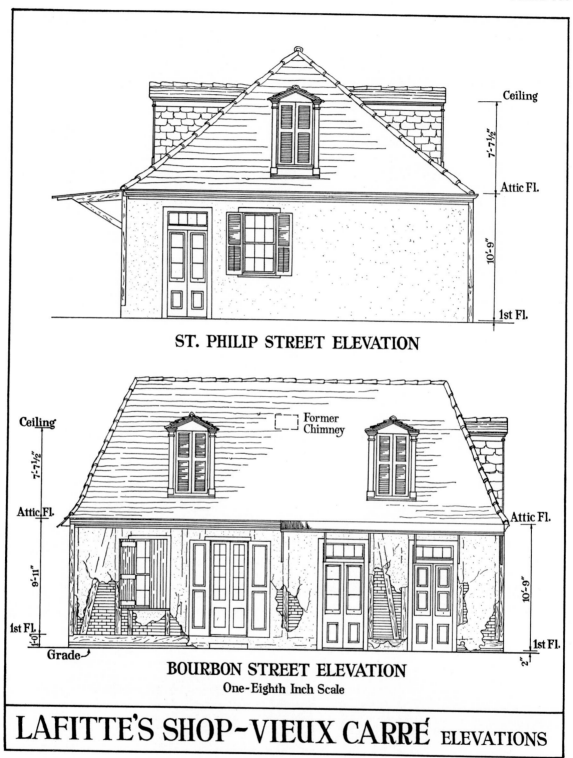

ST. PHILIP STREET ELEVATION

BOURBON STREET ELEVATION
One-Eighth Inch Scale

LAFITTE'S SHOP~VIEUX CARRÉ ELEVATIONS

House Illustrated, 1

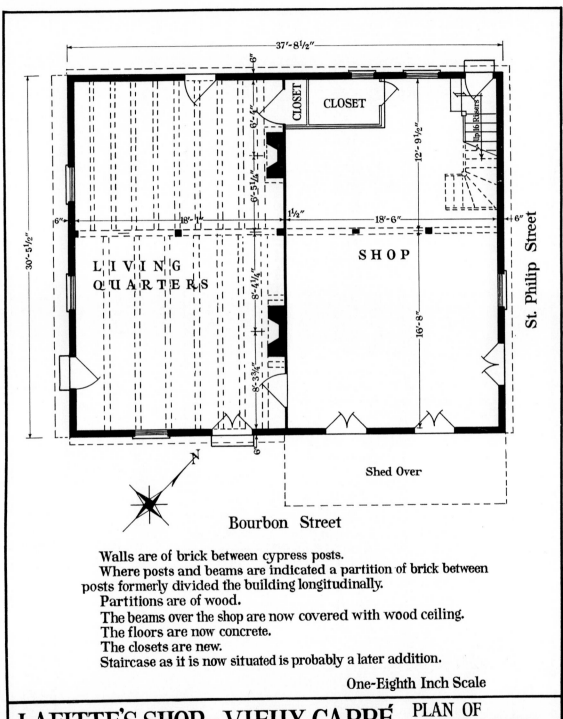

Walls are of brick between cypress posts.
Where posts and beams are indicated a partition of brick between posts formerly divided the building longitudinally.
Partitions are of wood.
The beams over the shop are now covered with wood ceiling.
The floors are now concrete.
The closets are new.
Staircase as it is now situated is probably a later addition.

One-Eighth Inch Scale

LAFITTE'S SHOP – VIEUX CARRÉ   PLAN OF GROUND FLOOR

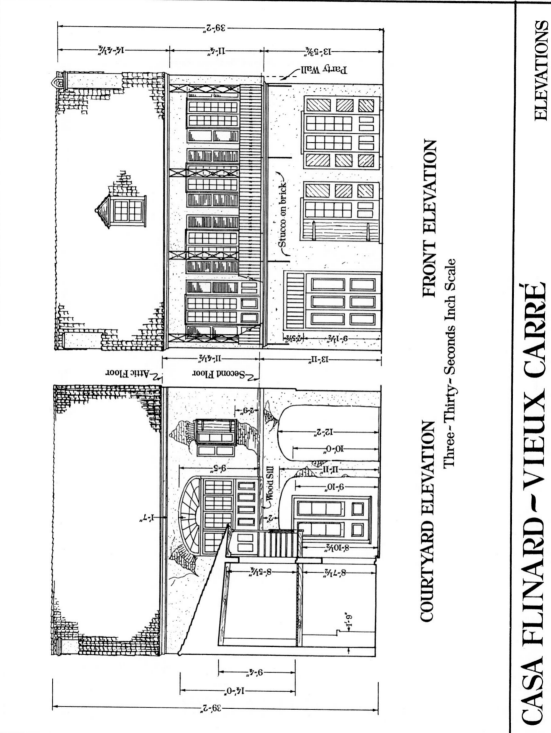

COURTYARD ELEVATION   FRONT ELEVATION

Three~Thirty~Seconds Inch Scale

CASA FLINARD~VIEUX CARRÉ

ELEVATIONS

Additional Illustrations, 10, 11, 83 and 88

Drawing of Mantel, 133

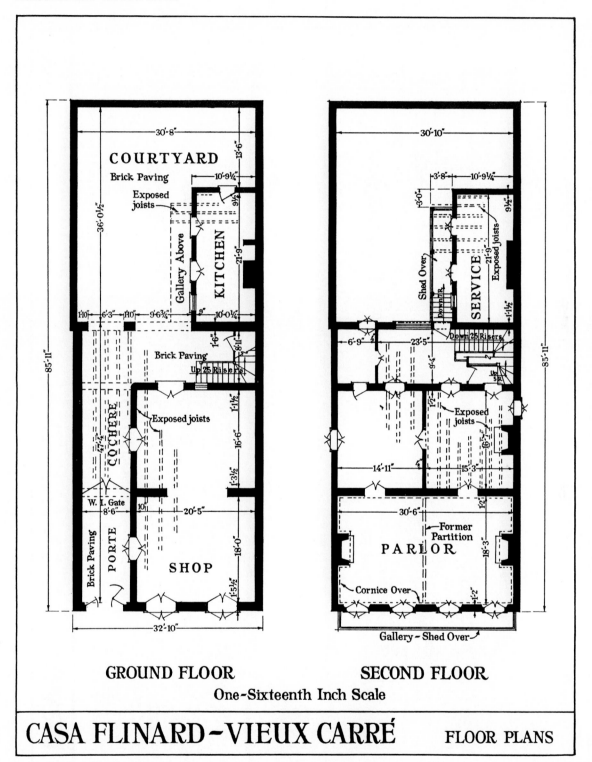

GROUND FLOOR   SECOND FLOOR
One-Sixteenth Inch Scale

CASA FLINARD~VIEUX CARRÉ   FLOOR PLANS

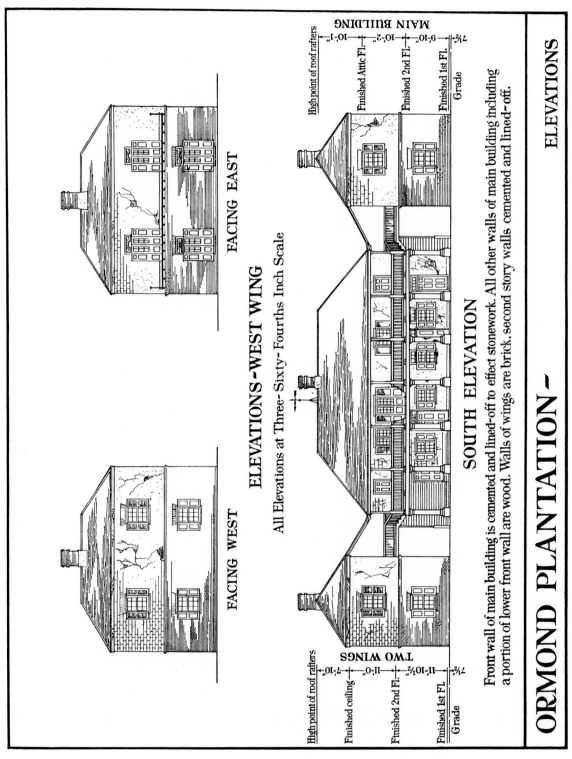

FACING EAST

FACING WEST

ELEVATIONS~WEST WING

All Elevations at Three~ Sixty~ Fourths Inch Scale

SOUTH ELEVATION

MAIN BUILDING

High point of roof rafters ‾ 10'-1"

Finished Attic Fl. ‾ 10'-2"

Finished 2nd Fl. ‾ 9'-10"

Finished 1st Fl. ‾ 7½"

Grade

TWO WINGS

High point of roof rafters ‾ 7'-10"

Finished ceiling ‾ 11'-0"

Finished 2nd Fl. ‾ 11'-10½"

Finished 1st Fl. ‾ 7½"

Grade

Front wall of main building is cemented and lined~off to effect stonework. All other walls of main building including a portion of lower front wall are wood. Walls of wings are brick, second story walls cemented and lined~off.

ORMOND PLANTATION~

ELEVATIONS

House Illustrated, 38
Additional Illustration, 40
Drawing of Staircase, 127

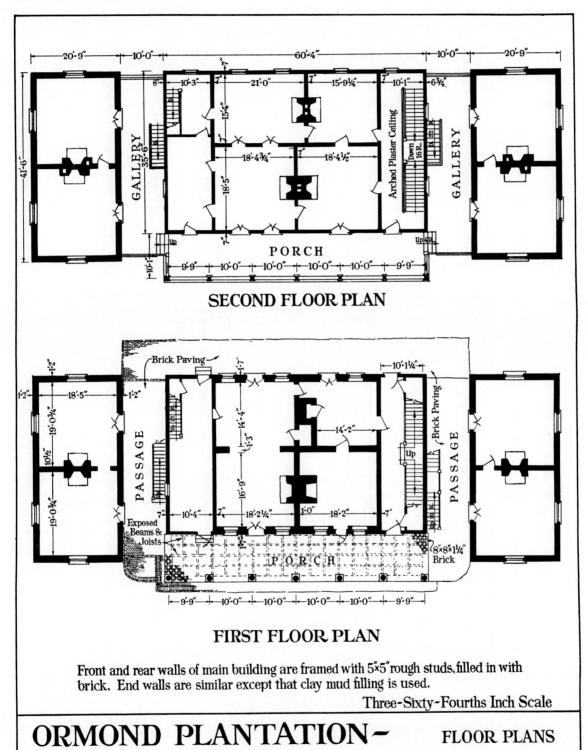

SECOND FLOOR PLAN

FIRST FLOOR PLAN

Front and rear walls of main building are framed with 5ˣ5ʺ rough studs, filled in with brick. End walls are similar except that clay mud filling is used.

Three-Sixty-Fourths Inch Scale

ORMOND PLANTATION~ FLOOR PLANS

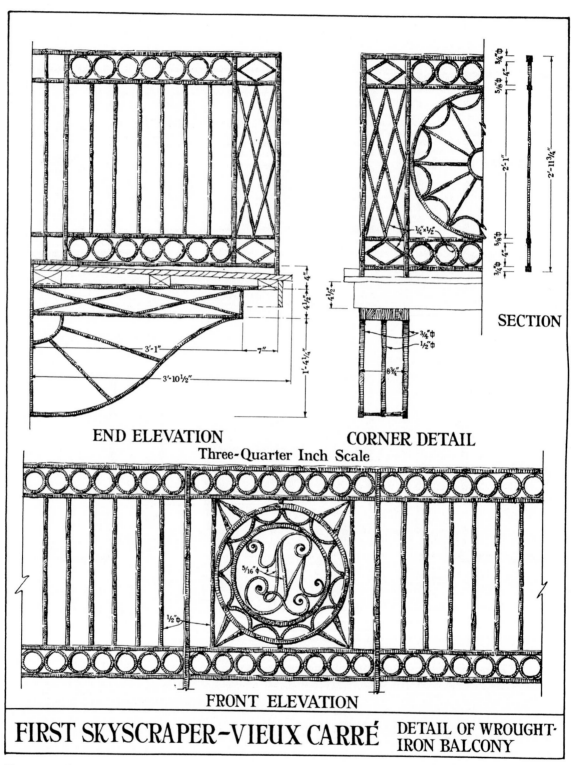

END ELEVATION

CORNER DETAIL

Three-Quarter Inch Scale

SECTION

FRONT ELEVATION

FIRST SKYSCRAPER—VIEUX CARRÉ

DETAIL OF WROUGHT-IRON BALCONY

Illustration, 51

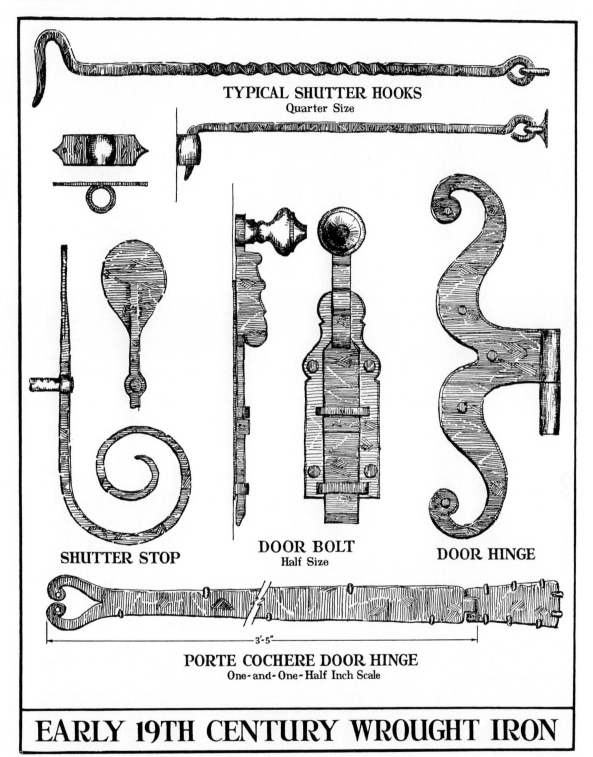

TYPICAL SHUTTER HOOKS
Quarter Size

SHUTTER STOP

DOOR BOLT
Half Size

DOOR HINGE

3'-5"

PORTE COCHERE DOOR HINGE
One-and-One-Half Inch Scale

EARLY 19TH CENTURY WROUGHT IRON

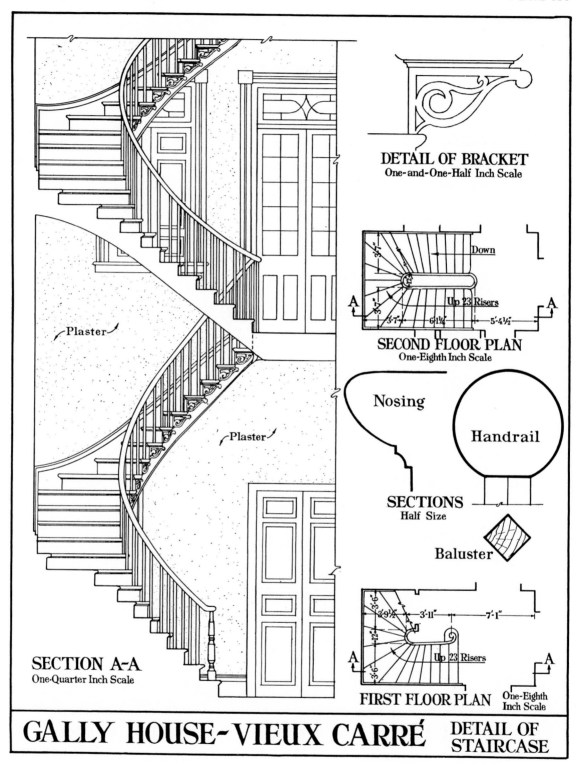

DETAIL OF BRACKET
One-and-One-Half Inch Scale

Down

A — Up 23 Risers — A

3'-7"   6'-1¼"   5'-4½"

SECOND FLOOR PLAN
One-Eighth Inch Scale

Nosing

Handrail

SECTIONS
Half Size

Baluster

Plaster

Plaster

SECTION A-A
One-Quarter Inch Scale

3'-6"
3'-9½"   3'-11"   7'-1"
4'-2"
A — Up 23 Risers — A
3'-6"

FIRST FLOOR PLAN   One-Eighth Inch Scale

GALLY HOUSE~VIEUX CARRÉ   DETAIL OF STAIRCASE

Additional Drawings, 131, 132 and 135

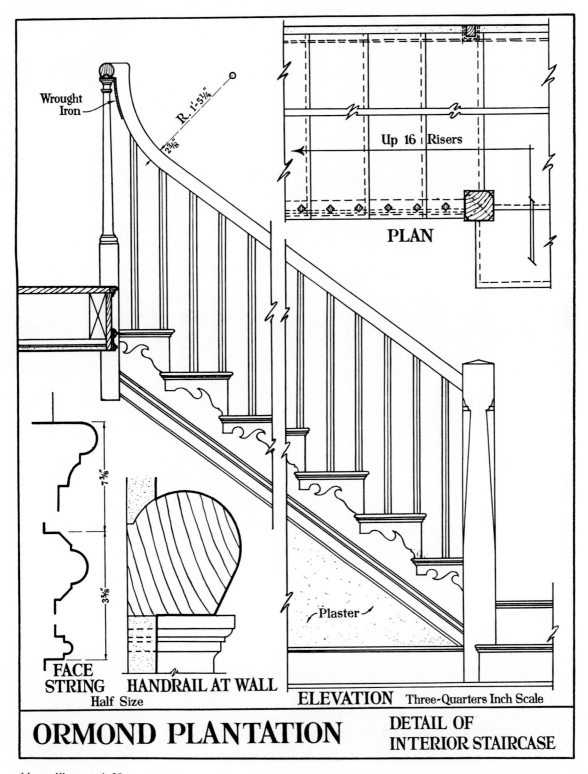

Wrought Iron

R. 1'-5¼"

2⅜"

Up 16 Risers

PLAN

7⅜"

3⅝"

Plaster

FACE STRING
Half Size

HANDRAIL AT WALL

ELEVATION Three-Quarters Inch Scale

ORMOND PLANTATION

DETAIL OF INTERIOR STAIRCASE

House Illustrated, 38
Additional Illustrations, 40
Additional Drawings, 122 and 123

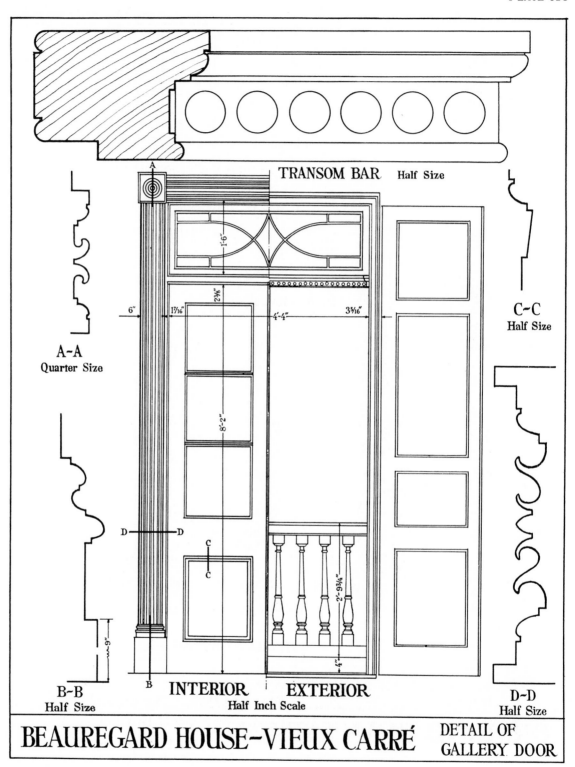

TRANSOM BAR   Half Size

A–A
Quarter Size

C–C
Half Size

B–B
Half Size

INTERIOR   EXTERIOR
Half Inch Scale

D–D
Half Size

BEAUREGARD HOUSE–VIEUX CARRÉ   DETAIL OF GALLERY DOOR

House Illustrated, 16
Additional Illustrations, 70 and 96

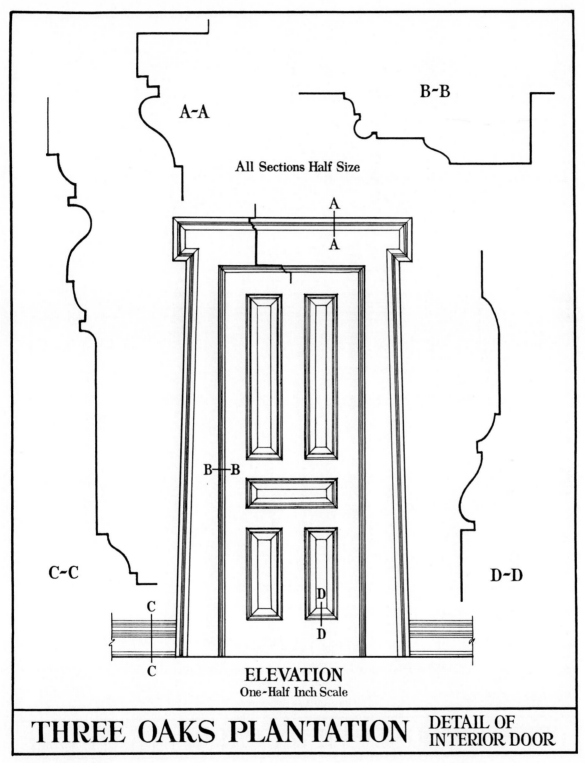

A-A

B-B

All Sections Half Size

A
A

B—B

C-C

D-D

C

D

C

D

ELEVATION
One-Half Inch Scale

THREE OAKS PLANTATION DETAIL OF INTERIOR DOOR

House Illustrated, 41
Additional Illustrations, 40 and 91

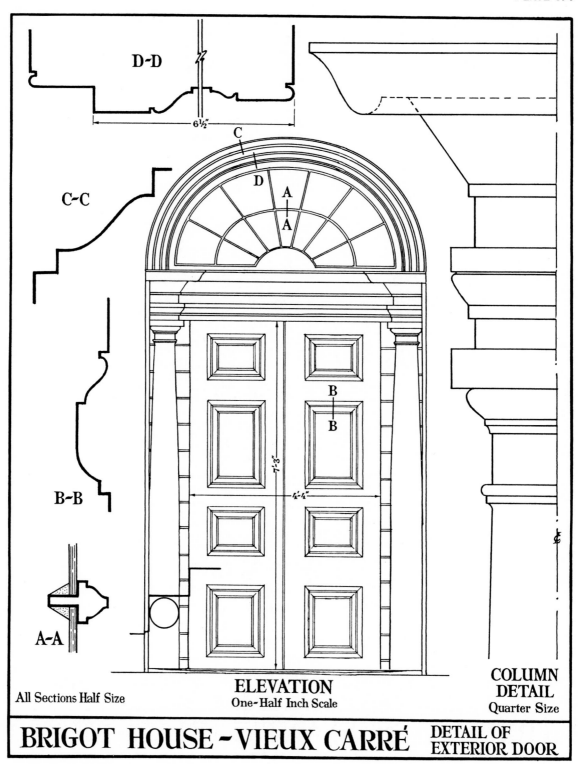

D-D

6½″

C-C

B-B

A-A

All Sections Half Size

C

D

A
A

B
B

7′-3″

4′-4″

ELEVATION
One-Half Inch Scale

COLUMN
DETAIL
Quarter Size

BRIGOT HOUSE - VIEUX CARRÉ   **DETAIL OF
EXTERIOR DOOR**

Doorway Illustrated, 68
Measured Drawing of Cornice, 134

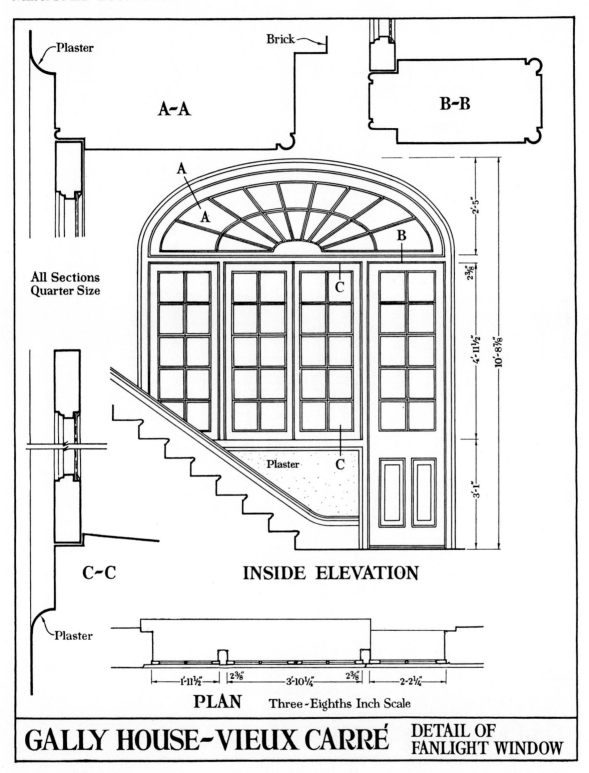

Plaster

Brick

A-A

B-B

All Sections
Quarter Size

A

A

B

C

C

Plaster

Plaster

C-C

INSIDE ELEVATION

2'-5"

2³⁄₈"

4'-11½"

10'-8⅞"

3'-1"

Plaster

1'-11½" 2³⁄₈" 3'-10¼" 2³⁄₈" 2-2¼"

PLAN   Three-Eighths Inch Scale

GALLY HOUSE-VIEUX CARRÉ   DETAIL OF
FANLIGHT WINDOW

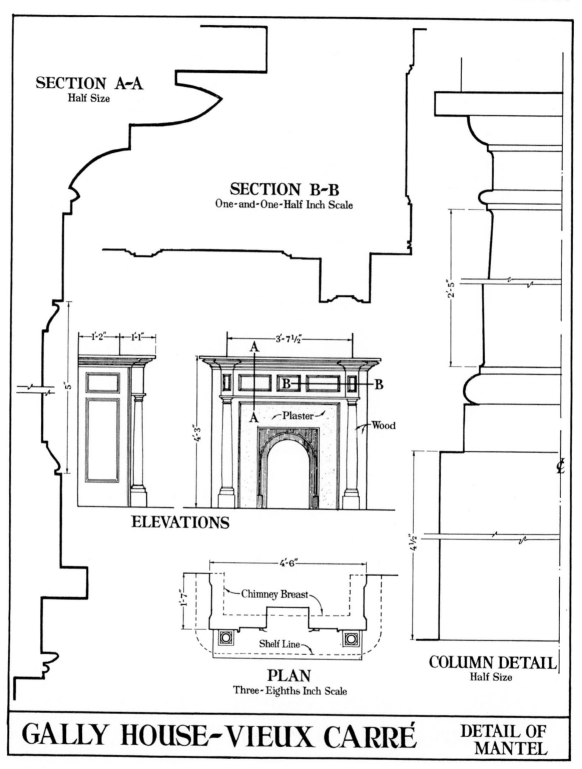

SECTION A-A
Half Size

SECTION B-B
One-and-One-Half Inch Scale

ELEVATIONS

PLAN
Three-Eighths Inch Scale

COLUMN DETAIL
Half Size

GALLY HOUSE-VIEUX CARRÉ

DETAIL OF
MANTEL

Measured Drawings, 126, 131 and 135

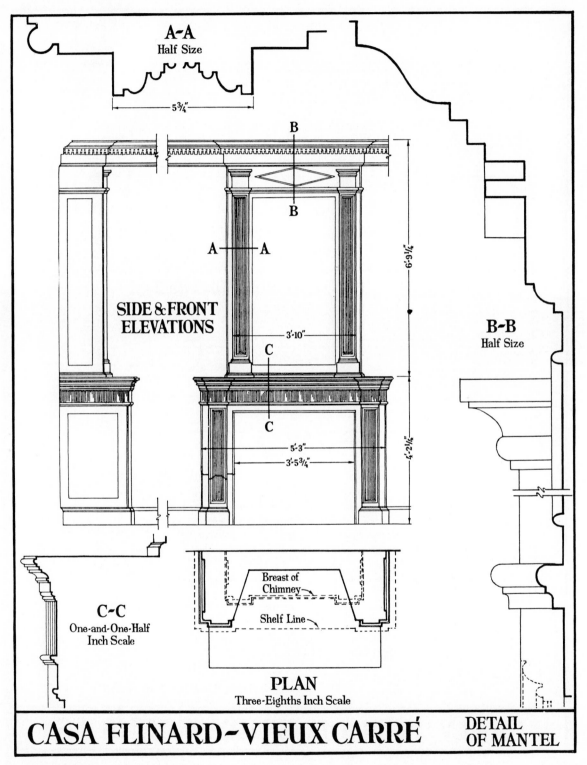

A-A
Half Size

5¾"

B

B

A————A

SIDE & FRONT ELEVATIONS

3'-10"

C

C

6'-9½"

4'-2½"

B-B
Half Size

5'-3"

3'-5¾"

C-C
One-and-One-Half Inch Scale

Breast of Chimney

Shelf Line

PLAN
Three-Eighths Inch Scale

CASA FLINARD – VIEUX CARRÉ

DETAIL OF MANTEL

Illustrated, 88

Additional Illustrations, 10, 11 and 83

Drawings, 120 and 121

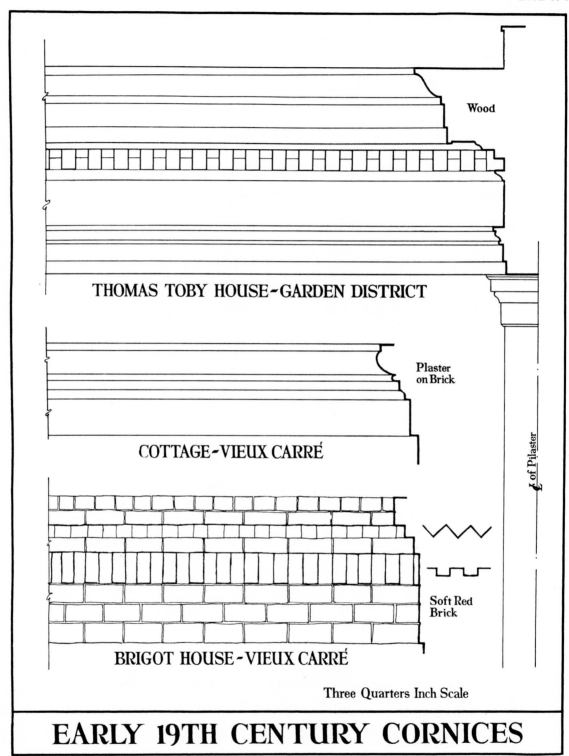

Wood

THOMAS TOBY HOUSE~GARDEN DISTRICT

Plaster on Brick

COTTAGE~VIEUX CARRÉ

℄ of Pilaster

Soft Red Brick

BRIGOT HOUSE~VIEUX CARRÉ

Three Quarters Inch Scale

EARLY 19TH CENTURY CORNICES

Illustrations of Thomas Toby House, 37 and 114
Illustration of Cottage in Vieux Carré, 3
Illustration of Doorway, Brigot House, 68
Additional Drawing, Brigot House, 130

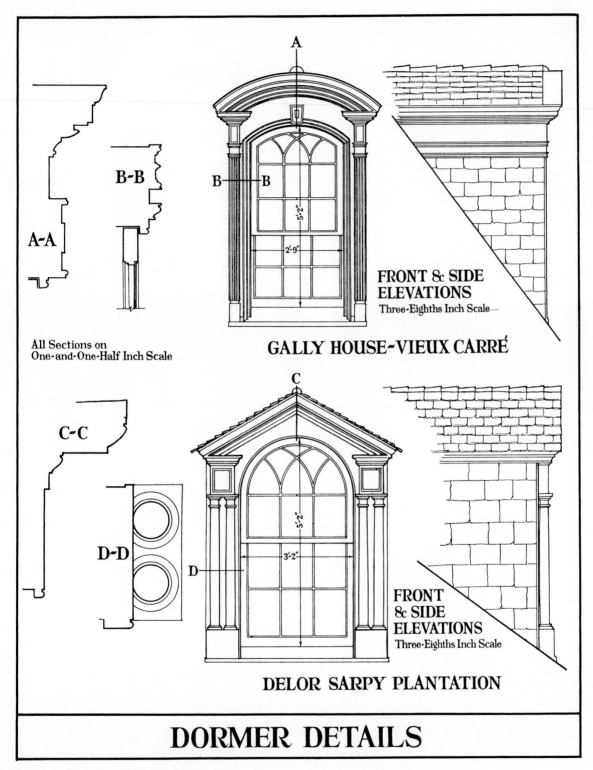

B-B

A-A

All Sections on
One-and-One-Half Inch Scale

FRONT & SIDE
ELEVATIONS
Three-Eighths Inch Scale

GALLY HOUSE~VIEUX CARRÉ

C-C

D-D

FRONT
& SIDE
ELEVATIONS
Three-Eighths Inch Scale

DELOR SARPY PLANTATION

DORMER DETAILS

Additional Drawings, Gally House, 126, 131 and 132
Dormer Illustrated, Delor Sarpy House, 108
Delor Sarpy House, Illustrated, 38

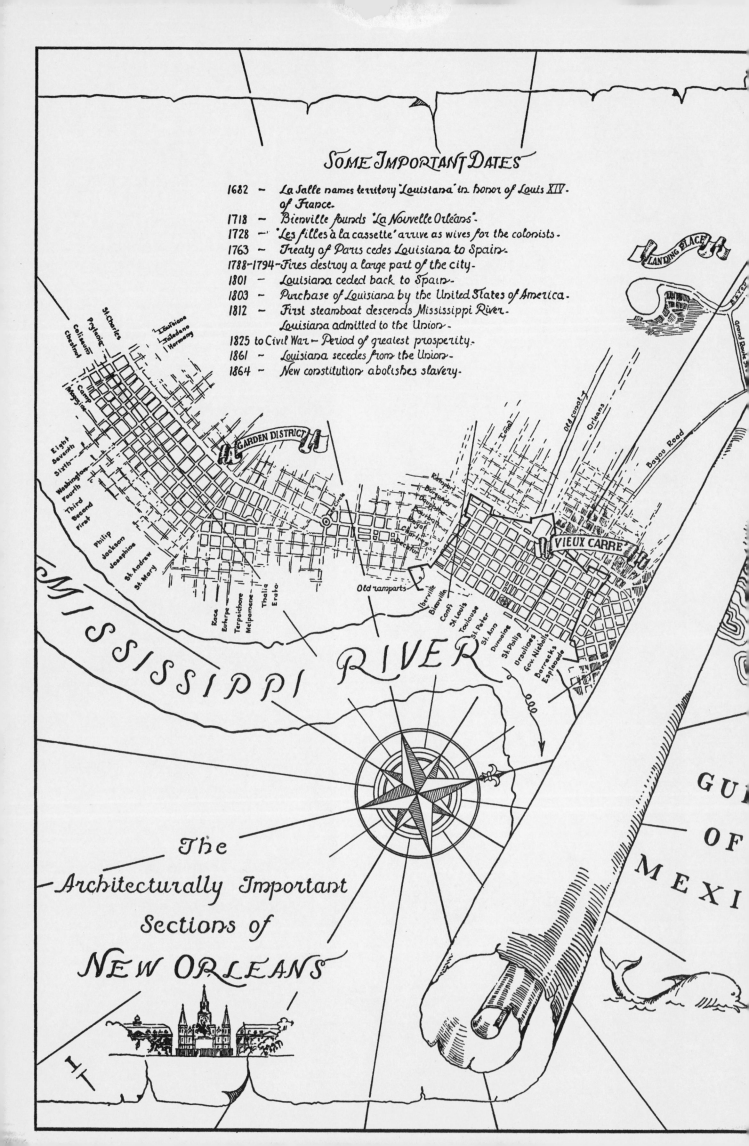

SOME IMPORTANT DATES

1682 — La Salle names territory "Louisiana" in honor of Louis XIV. of France.

1718 — Bienville founds "La Nouvelle Orléans".

1728 — "Les filles à la cassette" arrive as wives for the colonists.

1763 — Treaty of Paris cedes Louisiana to Spain.

1788-1794 — Fires destroy a large part of the city.

1801 — Louisiana ceded back to Spain.

1803 — Purchase of Louisiana by the United States of America.

1812 — First steamboat descends Mississippi River.
Louisiana admitted to the Union.

1825 to Civil War — Period of greatest prosperity.

1861 — Louisiana secedes from the Union.

1864 — New constitution abolishes slavery.

LANDING PLACE

GARDEN DISTRICT

VIEUX CARRE

MISSISSIPPI RIVER

GULF OF MEXI

The Architecturally Important Sections of NEW ORLEANS